The
QUEEN MOTHER'S
CENTURY

Robert Lacey

LITTLE, BROWN AND COMPANY
BOSTON NEW YORK LONDON

Art Director
Michael Rand

Contents

Childhood

Born on August 4, 1900, the future Queen Mother came in with the century, and part of her attraction was to carry through her life the grand and self-assured style of the Edwardian era in which she was raised. Elizabeth Angela Marguerite Bowes Lyon was the youngest-but-one of the Earl and Countess of Strathmore's ten children. She was not born royal, but nor was she ever just one of the people. On her father's side she could trace her ancestry to medieval Scottish warlords. Her mother was descended from the Duke of Portland, Prime Minister to King George III.

Glamis, where she spent her childhood summers, was the oldest inhabited castle in Scotland – the scene every August of shooting parties and fiercely contested cricket matches in which her father starred as a demon bowler. Her mother was famous for her candle-lit piano recitals after dinner, and she was also the driving force behind her daughter's lifelong love of history, literature and the arts. As Lady Strathmore recounted the legends of Glamis – the fabled home of Shakespeare's *Macbeth* – she kindled a poetic strand of mysticism in her daughter, along with an enduring belief in the importance of tradition.

The Strathmores were noted for their charm and eccentricity. 'They were so grand,' commented one friend, 'that you didn't notice that they were grand at all.' In London they had a house in St James's Square; in Hertfordshire their home was the rambling estate of St Paul's Walden Bury; and up in County Durham they had Streatlam Castle, set among the coalfields and iron deposits that were the source of the Bowes family's industrial wealth.

Living off, and caring for, an extended family of more than eight hundred estate workers and tenants, the Strathmores' existence of thoroughly-enjoyed privilege was imbued with a deep sense of obligation. 'Life is for living and working at,' read one of the needlework samplers that Elizabeth's mother loved to stitch. 'If anything or anyone bores you, then look for the fault in yourself.' To impose your own problems on others would be both arrogant and uncivilised, since being happy and spreading happiness were principal goals in a young lady's life.

Elizabeth Bowes Lyon, aged six, in the grounds of her family's Hertfordshire home at St Paul's Walden Bury

1900

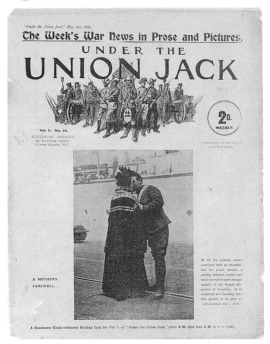

The Week's War News in Prose and Pictures.
UNDER THE
UNION JACK
Vol. II.—No. 26.
2D.
WEEKLY-

A MOTHER'S FAREWELL.

1901

Illustrated Mail.
THE EMPIRE MOURNS ITS LOSS.

She was dressed fluffily for her first photo (right), but when it came to posing (opposite), she was too shy to smile. Britain opened the century enmeshed in the Boer War (top), still raging when Queen Victoria died in 1901. Others born, like Elizabeth, with the century were jazz trumpeter Louis Armstrong, the Mercedes motorcar, the *Daily Express*, the hamburger (first put in a bun by Louis Lassen in his New Haven, Connecticut diner) – and the British Labour Party.

1902

Though youngest-but-one of the redoubtable Bowes-Lyon clan (above), Elizabeth had a presence of her own (right). In 1902 Britain celebrated King Edward VII's coronation (left), and the end of the Boer War, but had to come to terms with a new expression, 'concentration camp', the barbed-wire compound devised by the army to house the Boers driven from their farms. *Land of Hope and Glory* had its first performance, the first full transatlantic telegraph message was sent, and it was an excellent year for children's books: Kipling's *Just So Stories* , and Beatrix Potter's *Tale of Peter Rabbit.*

1903

On December 17, 1903, Orville Wright became the first man to fly – in the 605lb machine built with brother Wilbur in their North Carolina bicycle shop. Mrs Pankhurst founded the suffragettes, Marie Curie was the first woman to win a Nobel prize, for work on radio activity, and Pepsi-Cola was registered as a trade name. 'Coke' had already been around for seventeen years.

The closest companion of the four-year-old Elizabeth Bowes Lyon was her younger brother David (opposite and top left); her next best friend was her pony 'Bobs' (left, in front of Glamis). In 1904 Ivan Pavlov's salivating dogs won him a Nobel prize for his work on the 'conditioned reflex', the first electric 'Tube' train ran in London, and the theatrical hit of the year was the story of the boy who never grew up – J.M. Barrie's *Peter Pan.* Foreign affairs were dominated by Japan's victories over Russia in the Far East, deploying new technology – searchlights at night and wireless telegraphy.

11

By the age of six her winning pose had been perfected (right). Germany's Kaiser Wilhelm II was cheered through the streets when he visited London in 1907 (left), but the government still rejected plans for a Channel Tunnel on grounds of national defence. Baden-Powell held the first Boy Scout camp, and the Cunard liner *Lusitania* carried 873 passengers across the Atlantic in a record 4 days 19 hours and 52 minutes. Born in 1907: novelist Daphne Du Maurier, poet W.H. Auden and actor Laurence Olivier.

The Daily Mirror

THE MORNING JOURNAL WITH THE SECOND LARGEST NET SALE.

No. 1,479.   Registered at the G.P.O. as a Newspaper.   SATURDAY, JULY 25, 1908.   One Halfpenny.

DRAMATIC CLIMAX TO MARATHON RACE: FIRST MAN AT STADIUM HELPED HOME AND DISQUALIFIED.

There was a truly sensational climax in the Stadium yesterday to the great Marathon Race. By five o'clock there was hardly a vacant space to be seen, and the vast gathering had worked itself up to a state of breathless excitement. When the first man to reach the Stadium, who proved to be the Italian, Dorando, was seen to be practically exhausted, and fell four times in attempting to cover the prescribed distance round the track, the crowds were spellbound. Misguided enthusiasts helped him to rise, and actually escorted him to the tape, as seen above. This lost him the race, for Hayes (U.S.A.), who finished second, lodged a protest, which was upheld by the judges.

The hats had it – greeting friends at a garden party (right, with brother David and her mother beside her) and even when paddling (left) with David on the moors at Glamis. In 1908 London hosted the fourth Olympics at the White City, but over-helpful stewards sank gold medal chances for Italian Dorando Pietri (top). Veteran cricketer W.G. Grace retired after 43 years and 54,211 runs; in Manchester, Ernest Rutherford detected a single atom of matter; in Detroit, the Model T rolled off Henry Ford's production line. Born in 1908: conductor Herbert von Karajan and novelist Ian Fleming, creator of James Bond.

French aviator Louis Bleriot (top) took 43 minutes to travel from Calais to Dover – the first man to fly across the English Channel. Next year, the new power of radio was shown when wife-murderer Doctor Crippen (above) was arrested at sea while trying to flee to Canada. On January 1, 1909, Britain's first old-age pensions were paid – five shillings (25p) a week for everyone over 70 – and in 1910 Labour Exchanges opened for the unemployed. Edward VII died in 1910, to be succeeded by his son, George V, and in America the young motion picture industry made its first 'movie' in a sunny new location – the Los Angeles suburb of Hollywood.

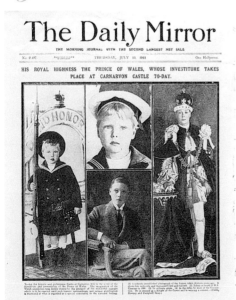

The 1911 investiture (far left) of George V's eldest son, Edward, as Prince of Wales marked a new royal generation. The world's largest and fastest liner, the 'unsinkable' *Titanic*, was the pride of the White Star line – until she went down (left) in April 1912 in the Atlantic, with the loss of more than 1,500 lives. 'Ragtime' was the hot new music from America, and *Alexander's Ragtime Band* was the hit of the year. At Glamis the nearly-teenage Elizabeth cuddled up to her elder brother Michael (above, to the right), one chilly afternoon before cricket.

1913

DAILY SKETCH.

HISTORY'S MOST WONDERFUL DERBY: FIRST HORSE DISQUALIFIED: A 100 TO 1 CHANCE WINS: SUFFRAGETTE NEARLY KILLED BY THE KING'S COLT.

The tragic death of suffragette Emily Davison (left) who threw herself in front of the King's horse, Anmer, in the 1913 Derby, was the culmination of a passionate votes-for-women campaign. Old hatreds rumbled in the Balkans, where conflicts between ethnic groupings intensified, prompting the meddling of outside powers which threatened to draw in the rest of Europe. Meanwhile a page from a family album shows Elizabeth and the Bowes Lyons enjoying the last summer of a golden world that was about to vanish for ever.

World War I

1914~1918

On August 4, 1914, the Lady Elizabeth Bowes Lyon went to the London Coliseum for a 14th birthday treat – box seats at a variety show featuring her favourite actor, Charles Hawtrey, and the ballerina Fedorova. But as the performers took their curtain call, the theatre manager walked onto the stage. Britain was now at war with Germany, he announced – and the theatre exploded in the wildest applause of the night.

'It all seemed so terribly exciting,' the Queen Mother later remembered. 'People throwing their hats in the air, shouting and cheering. The atmosphere was electric, and everyone couldn't wait to get at the enemy.' That night, as she lay in bed at 20 St James's Square, the fourteen-year-old could hear the huge crowds making their way down the Mall to cheer and congregate outside the gates of Buckingham Palace.

The Strathmores had no doubt where their duty lay. Elizabeth's four brothers of fighting age all enlisted for service, while Glamis Castle was converted into a reception centre and convalescent home for soldiers wounded at the front. The first casualties arrived in December 1914 and the Strathmore women set about the business of nursing and caring. If the first thirteen years of young Elizabeth's life inspired her conviviality and instinct for fun, the years 1914-18 helped develop her gritty determination and sense of service.

She took the walking-wounded for afternoon walks and picnics, and organised evening sing-songs for the bed-ridden in the hospital ward that had been converted from the castle's grand, oak-panelled dining room. She thought nothing of walking a mile each way to the village to get cigarettes and sweets for the convalescing guests of Glamis – the first people outside the Strathmore circle to fall under her spell. 'My three weeks at Glamis have been the happiest I ever struck,' declared one Scottish sergeant. 'As for Lady Elizabeth, why, she and my fiançay are as alike as two peas.'

Her caring came naturally, and was not staged to catch the eye of cameras or reporters. If you occupied a certain place in the world, it was just the sort of thing that you did.

Elizabeth Bowes Lyon wearing her nurse's uniform during World War I

The murder of Archduke Franz Ferdinand (above) brought war to Europe. For Elizabeth Bowes Lyon (right, with brother David and a convalescing officer), the 'war to end all wars' meant hospital duty – and personal tragedy. In September, 1915, a telegram brought news that her elder brother Fergus had been killed in the Battle of Loos. Earlier that year there had been more than 128 Americans among the 1,400 civilians drowned when the *Lusitania* (left) was torpedoed without warning by a German submarine. US involvement in the conflict drew closer.

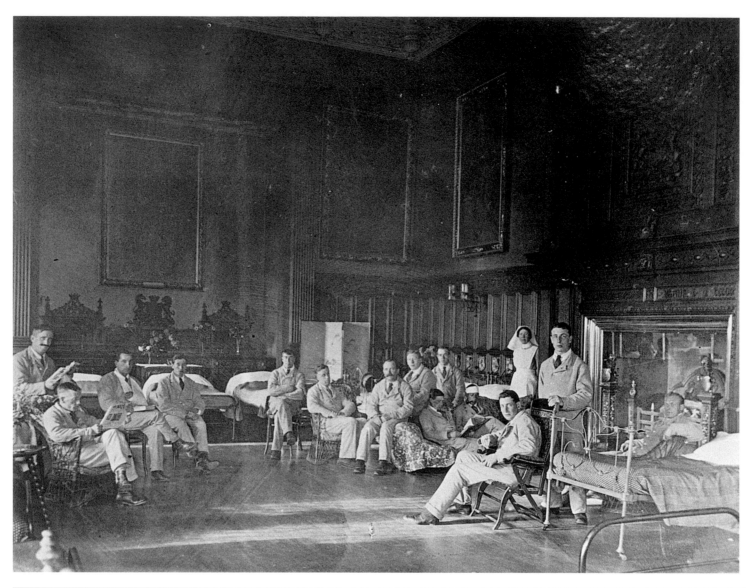

Ireland took advantage of the war to bid for independence in the Easter Uprising of 1916 (far left). In Russia (left), war casualties and starvation brought down the Czar. Anti-German feeling in Britain compelled the Royal Family to change their name from Saxe-Coburg-Gotha to Windsor; the Battenbergs became Mountbattens. Ten million enrolled as America entered the hostilities – and the wounded of Glamis (above) found a heroine in Lady Elizabeth Bowes Lyon (right).

The contribution that women made to victory in the Great War was recognised by giving women the vote, though this was restricted until 1928 to 'all women house-holders, house-holders' wives and women university graduates' who were over 30 years of age. A government commission was set up to further the next goal – equal pay for equal work. On the Western Front the use of tanks and planes hastened the end of trench warfare and brought about the surrender of Germany at 11am on the eleventh day of the eleventh month. More than ten million had died in the four and a quarter years of war – and the Bowes Lyons feared that brother Michael was among them when he was posted missing in action in the spring of 1917. In fact, Michael Bowes Lyon (see picture, p.106) was a prisoner of war, and arrived back in England on New Year's Eve, 1918, after a year and a half of captivity. Elizabeth's brother Jock also came home safely. But Patrick, the eldest brother and heir to the title, suffered from shell-shock, while brother Fergus lay buried in France, near the German redoubt that he died trying to capture in 1915.

Courtship

Upper-class Britain was both diminished and hardened by the slaughter of the Great War, and this loss of innocence was particularly obvious in young women. The bob-haired flapper of the Roaring Twenties smoked cigarettes, drank cocktails and lived for the moment with intimidating ferocity. But no one felt overawed by Elizabeth Bowes Lyon when she came down to London in 1919 to be formally introduced to society. She somehow stood aside from the rush of parties and fashionability which overwhelmed the post-war years. Elizabeth's style was, rather, wistful – ethereal even: 'mildly flirtatious in a very proper, romantic, old-fashioned, Valentine sort of way,' recorded the diarist Chips Channon. 'She makes every man feel chivalrous and gallant towards her.'

'Holding hands in a boat,' remembered Helen Cecil, her friend in those days, '*that* was her idea of courting.'

Elizabeth had no shortage of suitors, and the most persistent was Prince Albert, Duke of York, the shy and uncertain second son of King George V. 'Bertie' had suffered from a stammer since childhood, and lived in the shadow of his dashing and glamorous elder brother David, the Prince of Wales. But Bertie was a 'doer'. While David was to become famous for his expressions of concern over social injustice, it was Bertie who tried to make a difference. Reflecting on what it meant to live in the post-war world of social upheaval, he set up the Duke of York's Camps, where working-class youths and public schoolboys were brought together every summer in an effort to overcome class differences.

'You will be a lucky fellow if she accepts you,' was King George V's gruff response to the news of his second son's affection for Elizabeth, and so it proved. She turned Bertie down twice. Surrendering her privacy and freedom for the dubious chore of becoming royal was no great attraction to the very eligible daughter of a Scottish grandee.

As 1922 neared its close, the 27-year-old prince decided he would try again, and both families watched anxiously. 'I like him so much…' remarked Elizabeth's mother, Lady Strathmore. 'He is a man who will be made or marred by his wife.'

Debutante: a study of Elizabeth Bowes Lyon, aged 19, by the society photographer Van Dyke

The victorious allies gathered outside Paris at the Palace of Versailles (above), and spent five months seeking to piece together a better world order. The war had shattered four empires – Germany, Russia, Austria-Hungary and Ottoman Turkey – and from their debris arose an array of new 'nations'. Lithuania, Finland, Estonia and Latvia emerged around the Baltic, while down in the Balkans, Czechoslovakia and, later, Yugoslavia were constructed in hopes of smoothing the region's historic frictions. The world's first daily air passenger service was opened between London and Paris, and Nancy Astor became the first woman to sit in the House of Commons. The younger generation, still reeling from the war, felt entitled to some relaxation – and Elizabeth Bowes Lyon (right) was no exception. Anyone for tennis?

1920

Elizabeth Bowes Lyon was much in demand for brides-maid duty (left) – she brought such fun to the party. For the British government (below) the cycle of violence in Ireland was proving a challenge. In America, Prohibition dried up the nation's supplies of alcohol, and the New York Yankees paid a record $125,000 for baseball player Babe Ruth. London police were issued with cars instead of horses and the city of Norwich announced plans for a motorised travelling library. In France, the novels of former striptease artist Colette were the talk of Paris; in the US, *This Side of Paradise* by F. Scott Fitzgerald exposed fast set life in the Jazz Age.

The society photographer nudged aside the portrait painter in the 1920s, and in this study (left) by Hay Wrightson, Elizabeth Bowes Lyon showed herself the ideal subject. Between August and November the value of the German mark fell from 340 to the £1 to 1,200 (above) and, as unemployment grew worse, an obscure former army corporal, Adolf Hitler, was voted President of the National Socialist German Workers' Party. In Britain, churchmen and doctors protested at the opening by Dr Marie Stopes of the Mother's Clinic, the country's first birth control centre. A French aviator flew a helicopter for the first time; comedian Charlie Chaplin demonstrated his capacity for pathos in his first full-length film, *The Kid*; and the discovery of insulin offered hope for diabetics. Lovers of detective fiction were introduced to a new hero, Agatha Christie's Belgian sleuth, Hercule Poirot. Born on the island of Corfu in Greece, Prince Philip, future husband of Elizabeth II.

1922

In the summer of 1922, Elizabeth was photographed with Prince Albert, Duke of York (above, on the left); by the end of the year (right) she had pondered and turned down his two proposals of marriage. Labour won 142 seats in that year's general election (left), displacing the Liberals to become the official party of opposition to the Conservative government of Andrew Bonar Law; the BBC broadcast its first regular radio news bulletin. In Egypt, Tutankhamun's tomb was uncovered. Born in America: actress Judy Garland and *Reader's Digest*, a new magazine that was pocket-sized. As the Irish Free State came into existence, the last British troops packed their bags and marched out of Dublin.

Marriage

1923–1925

'ALL RIGHT BERTIE' read the telegram to Sandringham in the early weeks of January, 1923. It was Prince Albert's pre-arranged signal to his parents, the King and Queen, that his suit for Elizabeth had finally been successful. The news was made public on January 14. 'There is not a man in England today who doesn't envy him,' recorded Chips Channon in his diary. 'The clubs are in gloom.'

'I feel very happy, but quite dazed,' Elizabeth wrote to a friend after the engagement. 'We hoped we were going to have a few days' peace at first, but the cat is now completely out of the bag and there is no possibility of stuffing him back.'

The Duke of York was the first prince of the blood royal to marry in Westminster Abbey since Richard II wed Anne of Bohemia in 1382. But it was decided that the ceremony should not be broadcast by the recently created British Broadcasting Company. The Archbishop of Canterbury feared that men in pubs might be sipping beer while listening to the nuptials, and would fail to stand to attention when the National Anthem was played.

The press soon found a new name for Elizabeth – 'the smiling Duchess', or sometimes 'the little Duchess' because she was only five feet two inches tall – and she dived straight into public life. The summer of 1923 saw her taking over the patronage of the National Society for the Prevention of Cruelty to Children, and a few months later she was in Belgrade with her husband on their first trip abroad, attending the christening of the future King Peter II of Yugoslavia – heir to the kingdom of the Serbs, Croats and Slovenes.

Her sunniness brought cheer to the entire house of Windsor. One evening over dinner the Prince of Wales poured out his heart to Lady Diana Cooper. 'He described the gloom at Buckingham Palace,' recorded Lady Diana, 'how he himself and all of them froze up when they got inside it, how bad-tempered his father was: how the Duchess of York was the one bright spot there. They all love her and the King is in a good temper whenever she is there.'

Elizabeth, Duchess of York, in her wedding dress of antique ivory lace and chiffon moiré, embroidered with silver thread and pearls. It was made by the court dressmaker, Madame Handley Seymour

Elizabeth   Bertie

MARRIAGE OF

H.R.H. THE DUKE OF YORK, K.G.,

WITH

THE LADY ELIZABETH BOWES-LYON

IN WESTMINSTER ABBEY,

APRIL 26th, 1923.

LADY ELISABETH BOWES-LYON.

DAUGHTER OF LORD STRATHMORE BETROTHED TO THE DUKE OF YORK.

LADY ELISABETH BOWES-LYON,
Specially drawn for the "Daily Express" by Reginald Aird.

FRIEND AND BRIDESMAID OF PRINCESS MARY.

Court ☙ Circular.

York Cottage,
Sandringham,
January 15, 1923.

It is with the greatest pleasure that the King and Queen announce the betrothal of their beloved son, the Duke of York, to the Lady Elisabeth Bowes-Lyon, daughter of the Earl and Countess of Strathmore and Kinghorne, to which union the King has gladly given his consent.

The Duke of York, attended by Wing-Commander Louis Greig, has arrived at York Cottage.

BROTHERS' STORIES.
TOLD AT INTERVIEW WHEN OUT WITH THE GUNS.
From Our Special Correspondent.

FORFAR, Wednesday.

I found the Hon. David and the Hon. Michael Bowes-Lyon out with the guns at Glamis Castle, and showing evident satisfaction at the love match, which was not unexpected by them.

Both related interesting stories of Lady Elisabeth's youth.

On one occasion a party of Americans visited Glamis to see the ancient castle. Lady Elisabeth, hearing of their presence, immediately dressed herself as a housemaid and approaching the tourists offered to show them round and explain the historical associations.

They accepted, and on the completion of their tour thanked their guide and departed after tipping the daughter of the owner of the castle.

On the occasion of a visit to the Countess of Dalhousie's residence, Lady Elisabeth, accompanied by an aged stalker, named David Stormont, went away into the hills at Invermary, Forfarshire, to stalk deer. A heavy mist came down and both were lost. When the mist partially cleared they observed three handsomely antlered stags and Lady Elisabeth promptly killed them with Stormont's gun.

It was late in the evening that they returned to Lady Dalhousie's residence, weary but glad at their achievement.

Lady Elisabeth's chief recreations are fishing, tennis, golf, riding, and motoring. She has travelled extensively in France and Italy.

Mrs. John Bowes-Lyon.

BUCKINGHAM PALACE,
Thursday, 26th April, 1923.
WEDDING BREAKFAST.

Consommé à la Windsor.

Suprêmes de Saumon, Reine Mary.

Côtelettes d'Agneau, Prince Albert.

Chapons à la Strathmore.

Jambon et Langue découpés à l'Aspic.
Salade Royale.

Asperges, sauce Crème Mousseuse.

Fraises, Duchesse Elizabeth.
Paniers de Friandises.

Dessert.

Café.

In Britain, the first months of the year were dominated by the engagement of the King's second son to Elizabeth Bowes Lyon, portrayed (near left) in the soft-focus style of photographer Bertram Park. In a private family album (far left) Elizabeth's sister-in-law, Fenella, married to brother Jock, pasted a clipping which captured the popular excitement, along with the menu for the wedding breakfast, the Westminster Abbey order of service and the couple's first signed portrait together. The new Tory Prime Minister, Stanley Baldwin, called a December election (top) which resulted in a hung Parliament, but all parties agreed to postpone the crucial Commons votes – and Baldwin's resignation – so the nation could have a break from politics over Christmas. In Germany, children built play castles from piles of worthless banknotes. Born in 1923: soprano Maria Callas, statesman Henry Kissinger – and Chanel No 5, a scent from Coco Chanel, designer of the new liberated look for women. Passed in Britain, a divorce law permitting wives to sue for adultery: previously, only husbands had this right.

Thursday, April 26, 1923 dawned dull and rainy, but the weather had brightened perceptibly by 11 am when Elizabeth Bowes Lyon emerged (right) from her parents' London home to be driven by closed landau to Westminster Abbey. The antique Nottingham lace that made up her elegant, long bridal train had been borrowed from her future mother-in-law, Queen Mary.

Crowds cheered in the streets as the new Duchess of York rode with her husband (top) to Buckingham Palace. There the bride and groom gathered (left) for their wedding photo with no fewer than eight bridesmaids, following the precedent set by Queen Victoria in 1840. Also following Victorian precedent, the assembled group did not smile at the camera. Left to right: the Hon Diamond Hardinge, Lady Mary Cambridge (rear), the Hon Elizabeth Elphinstone (front), Lady Mary Thynne, Lady Katherine Hamilton, Lady May Cambridge (rear), the Hon Cecilia Bowes Lyon (front) and Miss Betty Cator. Elizabeth Elphinstone and Cecilia Bowes Lyon were nieces of the bride; the two Cambridge girls were relatives of Bertie; and the four other young women were all friends of Elizabeth.

On the first Sunday of their honeymoon they went to church (left) in the village of Bookham in Surrey. They were staying nearby at Polesden Lacey, a country home lent them by their friend the Hon Mrs Ronnie Greville, and they posed (above) on the rustic staircase in the lavishly landscaped gardens. 'I am quite certain,' wrote King George V to his newly married son, 'that Elizabeth will be a splendid partner in your work and help you in all you have to do.'

Stanley Baldwin resigned in January, and King George V put on a red tie to welcome Ramsay MacDonald (above), Britain's first Labour Prime Minister. In April Benito Mussolini led his Fascist 'black shirts' to a sweeping victory in Italy's general election and, as the year progressed, Joseph Stalin emerged in Russia as the most likely successor to Lenin, who had died at the beginning of the year. In America, 1924 was marked by George Gershwin's stunning jazz symphony, 'Rhapsody in Blue', by a craze for a grid-style brainteaser known as the crossword puzzle – and by the world's first gas-chamber execution. Born in 1924: filmstars Lauren Bacall and Marlon Brando, P.G.Wodehouse's *The Inimitable Jeeves*, and the first Winter Olympic Games. Edward, Prince of Wales (right, on the moors at Glamis beside his new sister-in-law, with brother Bertie behind) marked his thirtieth birthday by declaring that he would now start looking for a bride.

SPECIAL QUEEN ALEXANDRA MEMORIAL NUMBER

Daily Mirror

THE DAILY PICTURE NEWSPAPER WITH THE LARGEST NET SALE

8 PICTURE PAGES

No. 6,876   SATURDAY, NOVEMBER 21, 1925   One Penny

DEATH OF H.M. QUEEN ALEXANDRA
The Nation Mourns the Passing of a Loved and Gracious Lady

The gentle and much-loved Queen Alexandra (above), widow of Edward VII, died at Sandringham in November, aged 80. Greeting a wounded soldier in the Royal Botanic Gardens at Kew (right), the House of Windsor's latest recruit brought her own informality and lightness to the royal style. In South Africa the Afrikaaner-dominated government proposed passing the 'colour bar' into law, and in Germany Hitler published his best-selling racial diatribe, *Mein Kampf*. A new sort of inn opened in California – the 'motel' which accommodated cars as well as guests – while in Tennessee a schoolteacher, John Scopes, was fined $100 for teaching his pupils the theory of evolution. Born in 1925: black activist Malcolm X, Goon Peter Sellers, Margaret Roberts (the future Prime Minister, Mrs Thatcher) – and the electric clothes-washing machine. Art critics declared that the decade had found its stylistic 'voice' in a clean and angular design tradition later known as Art Deco.

Family Life

1926 – 1935

It was as a mother that she really came into her own. Her first daughter, Elizabeth, was born in 1926, and Margaret Rose arrived four years later. They were the first new princesses of the century – and the first royal children to be subjected to the scrutiny of the masses and their media. So great was public curiosity that the baby Elizabeth's pram excursions in Green Park had to be abandoned.

The family lived right beside the park at 145 Piccadilly in a home that was grand by most people's standards, but was anything but a palace. Bertie and Elizabeth enjoyed the life of an urban young couple of the 1920s, slipping out to the cinema and restaurants without ceremony. When the young Elizabeth and Margaret Rose walked out of their front door, they stepped into a street thronged with buses and people.

The Duchess of York made shrewd use of this comparative normality. In the published accounts of her family life she proved to have a deft and contemporary instinct for image management. Best-selling volumes 'written and published with the *personal approval* of Her Royal Highness' took readers into the nursery of 145 Piccadilly to hear the happy screams and splashes from the little princesses' bathroom. The two girls were educated at home by a governess – going to a school with ordinary children would have been far too modern. But their mother's belief that the girls' education should be spontaneous, playful and, above all, fun was very much in line with the new ways of teaching pioneered in these years by such reformers as Montessori.

Weekends were spent at Royal Lodge in Windsor Great Park, with a full complement of dogs and ponies. It was a comfortable existence, far removed from the realities of the Great Crash, the Depression, and some of the century's toughest years. The Duchess of York's first priority was her family – and, in particular, the fortifying of her shy husband. As the reign of the King George V drew to a close, the behaviour of his eldest son, Edward Prince of Wales, was becoming a matter of grave concern to his family. For all sorts of reasons, it was important to have a strong team in reserve.

The Duchess of York, with her daughters Princess Elizabeth (far right) and Princess Margaret Rose, arriving at Olympia for the Royal Tournament in 1935

In New York, thousands of sobbing women threw themselves at the coffin of movie heart-throb Rudolph Valentino (above). Aged 31, the smouldering star of *The Sheikh* had died of complications from a ruptured appendix. In England, popular interest focused on the birth of the Duke and Duchess of York's first child, Princess Elizabeth (right and far right, on the day of her christening, May 26). Born in the same year as the princess: jazz musician Miles Davis, film star Marilyn Monroe, and A.A. Milne's disarming 'bear of little brain', Winnie-the-Pooh. Britain was convulsed by a General Strike, but in Italy Mussolini passed a law that made all strikes illegal. Beside the Red Sea, King Ibn Saud completed his conquest of Arabia and named his new country after himself and his family – Saudi Arabia. In Germany, the Nazi party found a boss for its Berlin branch, philosophy professor Dr Josef Goebbels.

49

1927

In January the Duke and Duchess of York set sail (above) for Australia to open the new Parliament building, leaving nine-month-old Elizabeth (right) behind. 'It quite broke me up,' the Duchess confessed – but once on board HMS *Renown* she organised vigorous deck activities and became dance mistress to the ship's company. The tour meant that the young mother missed her baby's first words and first birthday, but it was in Australia that Bertie finally triumphed over his painful stammer, thanks to the breathing exercises that he practised with Elizabeth. As the couple steamed home in May, US aviator Charles Lindbergh was heading for France (left) in the first ever solo Atlantic flight. In London, the Park Lane Hotel opened, Britain's first to offer a bathroom with every bedroom – and October saw the US premier of *The Jazz Singer*, the first talking picture. Promised Al Jolson, the movie's star: 'You ain't heard nuttin' yet!'

1928

1929

People had more fun than ever (far left), as the 1920s moved to a close, but there were strikes in England, and in America the Wall Street Crash of October 1929 (left) wiped out the life savings of millions. Elizabeth kept up her schedule of public engagements (above, in Aberdeen with Bertie), and (right) visiting Ilford in Essex, where well-wishers gave her a teddy-bear to take home for baby 'Lillibet'. Born in 1928: the cartoon character Mickey Mouse, just a year older than the spinach-eating Popeye (b. 1929).

1930

Australian batsman Donald Bradman (below) rewrote the record books at the expense of England's hapless cricketers. It was some distraction from economic catastrophes which saw the pound devalued by 30 percent (bottom). For the York family, 1930 brought the birth of a second daughter, Margaret Rose, displayed (right) at a Glamis garden party. Born in the same year: Clint Eastwood, Sean Connery and a synthetic fabric known as 'nylon'. In November, 1931, Mahatma Gandhi scandalised George V and Queen Mary when he arrived for tea at Buckingham Palace wearing a loin cloth.

1931

1932

Britain's Malcolm Campbell beat his own land speed record when he touched 267 mph at Florida's Daytona Beach. US unemployment reached 1.6 million, and polio victim Franklin Delano Roosevelt won a presidential landslide when he promised Americans a 'New Deal'. In Britain a bill was introduced to end the whipping of children under 14 as a legal punishment. King George V made his first Christmas broadcast.

1933

'I think this would be a good time for a beer,' declared President Roosevelt as he ended America's 'dry' years. In Germany opposition parties were banned and Jews were sent to the first concentration camp at Dachau, outside Munich. Oxford students voted 275 to 153 that they would 'in no circumstances' fight for King and country. Moviegoers shivered at King Kong, and singer Marlene Dietrich started a fashion trend for women – the wearing of men's suits.

1934

Within three hours of the August death of President Hindenberg, Adolph Hitler had taken over his powers (left). Germans approved the new status of the Führer ('Chief' or 'Leader') by 38 million votes to 4 million, and gathered in Nuremberg to cheer the prospect of a German Reich ('Empire') that would last a thousand years; the compulsory sterilisation of physically 'imperfect' citizens became German law, and Nazi clergy rewrote the Psalms to exclude references to the Jews. In England the summer rituals of the Derby and Ascot (top and right) continued, but Winston Churchill warned of the weakness of the country's defences. In America, maverick gangsters Bonnie Parker and Clyde Barrow died in a hail of police bullets. Born in 1934: film stars Brigitte Bardot and Sophia Loren. In China, the Communist leader Mao Tse-tung began his army's Long March to escape the nationalist forces of General Chiang Kai-shek.

1935

The protests of the League of Nations were shrugged off by Mussolini (left) as Italian tanks and planes attacked the primitive feudal kingdom of Ethiopia (Abyssinia). The growing arrogance of the Fascist powers persuaded Britain to start re-arming: it was announced that the number of planes in the RAF would be increased three fold over the course of the next two years, and that gasmask production would be stepped up to meet the needs of civil defence. But the summer was taken up with the happier series of Silver Jubilee events that celebrated King George V's 25 years on the throne. At London's Olympia (top), the Yorks joined the crowds watching the circus, and off the Isle of Wight (opposite), the Duke and Duchess sailed with the Royal Thames Yacht Club in the Jubilee Regatta. Loyalty to the crown stood higher than ever – but it was the old king's last summer.

Abdication

1936

King Edward VIII was blessed with star quality, and the adulation that he generated mirrored the worship attending America's new royalty, the screen idols of Hollywood. His informality was disarming and he was an attentive uncle to the princesses, Elizabeth and Margaret Rose. But they saw less and less of him as his affection deepened for an American divorcee, Wallis Simpson, and with that fateful relationship, the British monarchy – and the life of Elizabeth, Duchess of York – changed for ever.

'Ma'am,' confided Stanley Baldwin sadly to the new sovereign's mother, Queen Mary, 'the King has no religious sense.' The Prime Minister was trying to define the package of values needed to underpin a successful constitutional monarch – a subtle formula in which good looks and glamour alone are not enough. Humility, duty and an instinct for the intangible are needed in those who would be royal icons.

Religion certainly mattered deeply to the Yorks. When Bertie and Elizabeth first realised how the new king's infatuation might deprive him of his throne, they were reported to have gone down on their knees in prayer. For them, royalty was a holy and mystical trust.

Edward VIII's Act of Abdication, signed on December 11, 1936, was a sharp lesson in constitutional reality. The monarch had been sent packing because his personal will had come into conflict with that of his elected government, and this humiliation had been compounded by the disappointment which many felt at the former king's wayward personal behaviour. A spell had been broken.

It fell to Elizabeth and her husband to restore the magic – and the more serious and steely side of the smiling Duchess became apparent. In later years, people were to make much of the anger with which, it was said, she condemned her brother-in-law and the woman for whom he gave up his throne: the pair had jeopardised the monarchy and cast an unfair burden on poor Bertie's shoulders. But the more creative aspect of Queen Elizabeth's strength lay in the comfort and support with which she built up her husband, the new king. Wallis Simpson had deconstructed her man – but Elizabeth proved the making of hers.

'Uncle David' – Prince of Wales, King Edward VIII and, finally, Duke of Windsor – with his nieces the Princesses Elizabeth (left) and Margaret Rose

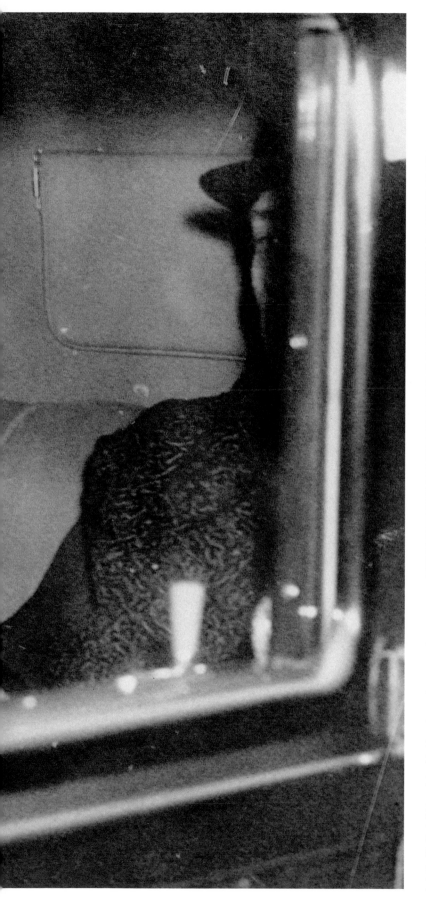

King George V died on January 21, 1936, and the next day the Duke and Duchess of York travelled (left) to escort his coffin from Sandringham to London. They had no idea that they would become King and Queen by the end of that year, but King Edward VIII's insistence that he could not rule 'Without the help and support of the woman I love' brought his brief and unhappy reign to an end by December. Britain's Year of Three Kings also saw the Civil War start in Spain, with General Franco at the head of the rebel forces. Jesse Owens won four gold medals for America at the Berlin Olympics, to the ill-disguised fury of Adolf Hitler. Gatwick Airport opened – and after two years of experiments with silent pictures, the BBC succeeded in adding sound, thus inaugurating the world's first public television service. Rudyard Kipling, poet and muse of the Empire, died aged 70, while new births included Swiss actress, Ursula Andress, and French designer, Yves St Laurent – along with Britain's board-game of the year: if you could get hold of both Mayfair and Park Lane, you were sure to be a champion at Monopoly.

Coronation

The new king, George VI, and Queen Elizabeth spent months preparing for their coronation, concluding with a meeting with the Archbishop of Canterbury in Buckingham Palace. 'They knelt with me,' the Archbishop recorded. 'I prayed for them and for their realm and Empire, and I gave them my personal blessing. I was much moved, and so were they. Indeed, there were tears in their eyes when we rose from our knees.'

People who were close to the new king and queen in Westminster Abbey felt they could sense a sacramental aura coming off the couple, and the king himself subsequently confided to Ramsay MacDonald that he had, at times, been in something of a trance.

Talking later with the Queen, MacDonald remarked on how well the King was performing in his new role, and Elizabeth was delighted. 'And am I doing all right?' she asked. 'Oh you...' the former Prime Minister replied, and he gave a sweep of his arm to indicate that, in her, he just took that for granted.

In the late 1930s the new Queen Elizabeth not only healed the wounds of abdication. In a series of dramatically popular foreign tours to France and North America, she developed a fresh, approachable style of public royal behaviour. In the process of laying a foundation stone on a visit to Canada in the late 1930s, she heard that some of the stonemasons among the watching workers came from Scotland, and she stepped out boldly away from the official party and into the crowd in order to talk to them. It was the first example of the modern informal 'walkabout'.

When the royal couple arrived back in London from their tour later that year, the House of Commons broke off its debate and the MPs came out on the pavement to greet them. 'We lost all our dignity and yelled and yelled,' reported Harold Nicolson, the author and critic who represented West Leicester for the National Labour Party . 'The Queen was superb. She really does manage to convey to each individual in the crowd that he or she has had a personal greeting... She is in truth one of the most amazing queens since Cleopatra.'

King George VI and Queen Elizabeth with the Princesses Elizabeth and Margaret Rose in their coronation robes, May 12, 1937. Overleaf: Queen Elizabeth watches her husband at the moment of crowning in Westminster Abbey

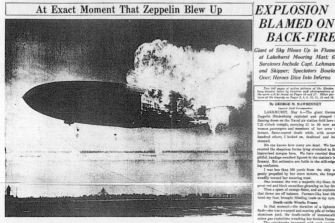

The May 6 explosion of the German airship Hindenburg (above) as she came in to land in New Jersey effectively ended this form of air travel. A week later the eyes of the world focused on London, where the newly crowned King George VI, Queen Elizabeth and their daughters (right) acknowledged the cheers of the crowds: BBC cameras captured the day's processions in Britain's first television outside broadcast. In San Francisco motorists drove for the first time over the new, 4,200 ft Golden Gate Bridge, the world's longest. In the Spanish Civil War, the Basque capital of Guernica was savagely bombed and burned by German planes sent by Hitler to help General Franco, and within weeks Pablo Picasso had painted his vast, nightmare canvas of the atrocity. Britain stirred controversy with plans to create a national homeland for the Jews in Arab Palestine. In China, the warring leaders Mao Tse-tung and General Chiang Kai-shek united in the face of attack from Japan. Making her debut in *Giselle*, 18-year-old Peggy Hookham became the star of London's ballet world, her stage name – Margot Fonteyn.

Mass rejoicing greeted Britain's Prime Minister Neville Chamberlain (above), when he returned from Munich holding an agreement which, he said, brought home 'peace with honour'. Next day, Nazi troops marched into Czechoslovakia under the terms of the agreement – shameful appeasement, in the eyes of such critics as Winston Churchill. Earlier in the year, George VI and his wife had visited Paris to strengthen Anglo-French solidarity, and Queen Elizabeth had dazzled the fashion-conscious capital with her romantic cobweb-white dress and parasol. A Cecil Beaton photo-session later re-created the spectacle (right) in the gardens of Buckingham Palace. In Russia, Stalin staged show trials in which party colleagues confessed to unbelievable crimes of treason, and were executed. In America, radio listeners were thrown into panic by Orson Welles's *War of the Worlds* 'reporting' the landing of Martians in New Jersey. On a highway in Indiana, the breathalyser was born. But as the year ended, Europe was dominated by Adolf Hitler and his ambitions for his thousand year Reich.

Finest Hour

1939~1945

When World War II broke out in September 1939, Queen Elizabeth started taking revolver lessons. 'I shall not go down like the others,' she declared stoutly – the 'others' being the royal families of Continental Europe, overrun in short order by the armies of Nazi Germany.

King George VI and Queen Elizabeth led their people through a new kind of war. Opting to share in the privations endured by the rest of the country, they spent their nights in air raid shelters, painted a five-inch-high ring round the inside of their bathtub to restrict the wastage of water, and suffered omelettes composed of powdered egg. When offered a substantial meal on a tour of bomb-damage in Lancashire, Queen Elizabeth remarked to the local mayor that, back at the Palace, they were very particular about observing the rationing regulations.

'Oh well then, Your Majesty,' returned His Worship, 'you'll be glad of a proper do.'

The Queen decided that uniform was not for her, but nor would she wear anything black or sombre. In war, as in peace, it was her job to be recognisable and to raise spirits, and thus was created the reassuring silhouette, topped off with a hat, that would forever symbolise Queen Elizabeth the Queen Mother. The plump little figure picking her way through the rubble, bringing comfort with her and an unfailing smile, came to sum up many people's fonder memories of the Second World War. One day in London a woman was trying to coax her terrified dog out of her bombed home.

'Perhaps I can try,' suggested the Queen. 'I am rather good with dogs.'

As things turned out, she never needed to fire her revolver in earnest – and she could take some of the credit for that. 'This war,' wrote Winston Churchill in 1941, 'has drawn the throne and the people more closely together than was ever before recorded.' One American newspaper described Queen Elizabeth as Britain's 'Minister for Morale'. Through five years of nerve and steadiness, her charisma and personal example were key ingredients in her country's drive for victory. It was Britain's finest hour, and also hers.

Queen Elizabeth visits children sleeping in an air-raid shelter in the East End of London

1939

WAR DECLARED ON GERMANY

Britain's Ultimatum Ignored By Hitler

FRANCE WILL FIGHT TOO, CHAMBERLAIN TELLS EMPIRE

The Queen's Working Party (above) was a group of Buckingham Palace staff who gathered from September 1939 onwards to knit and stitch for the war effort. Mixing glamour with practicality, the Queen posed (right) for the royal Christmas card, sent to every man and woman in the armed forces. By the end of the year, sugar, meat, butter and bacon were all rationed and 1.5 million children had been evacuated from Britain's towns and cities. In America, nylon stockings went on sale for the first time and Glenn Miller's *In the Mood* was top of the hit parade. Judy Garland, 17, became a star overnight in *The Wizard of Oz*. The French abolished public executions. An all-male Oxford college (Balliol) elected a woman to a fellowship for the first time, and Sigmund Freud died in London. Germaine Greer was born in Australia.

ILLUSTRATED 3ᵈ

AIR RAID LIVES
—Exclusive Pictures

BOMBING OF BUCKINGHAM PALACE—see inside

It was March before the first British civilian was killed in a German air-raid, but by September the Luftwaffe was raining bombs on London, including Buckingham Palace (above). 'I am glad we have been bombed,' said Queen Elizabeth. 'It makes me feel we can look the East End in the face.' She and her husband went straight to the Cockney heartlands (right), and were to form a morale-boosting team with Winston Churchill, who in May succeeded Neville Chamberlain as Prime Minister. In June, France surrendered and German soldiers were issued with English phrase books in preparation for their next conquest. Himmler issued secret orders for the building of concentration camps at Auschwitz, while the Vichy government in France quietly lent French assistance to Hitler's anti-semitic policies. *Gone With The Wind* swept the Oscars at America's Academy Awards and John Steinbeck won a Pulitzer Prize for *The Grapes of Wrath*. Golfer Jack Nicklaus was born in January. February saw the death of John Buchan, author of *The Thirty-Nine Steps*.

Japan's December assault on the US Navy in Pearl Harbor (above) was to prove the turning point of World War II, swinging America's massive firepower and resources behind the Allies, for whom 1941 had been tough going. In April, British income tax rose to a record 50 per cent to pay for the £11 million-a-day cost of hostilities, and Germany extended its military hold over Greece and North Africa. May bombing raids reduced the House of Commons to rubble, along with much of the City of London. German Panzer divisions swept into Russia. The gallant island of Malta suffered its 1,000th air raid. Fifteen hours and 48 minutes of solid sunshine made July 6 Britain's sunniest day of the century, and the picture of Queen Elizabeth and her daughters (left) enjoying the weather 'somewhere in the country' was a deliberately upbeat change from images of the royal family visiting scenes of destruction. It was well known that the Queen had turned down suggestions that the girls should seek safety in Canada. 'They will not leave me,' she said. 'I will not leave the King – and the King will never leave.'

Marines Crush Jap Attack
16 Pages of Comics + 16 Page Color Magazine

WALL ST. Journal American 5¢
SPECIAL

800,000 NAZIS MASSED AT STALINGRAD!

Queen Elizabeth toured a munitions factory (near right), inspected the work of a land girl (below) and visited a London canteen for bomb victims (far right). In January, secret Nazi discussions moved the 'Final Solution' a step nearer, and in March the first Jews were deported to Auschwitz. But by the end of the year Rommel's elite divisions were on the run from Britain's General Montgomery and his 'Desert Rats' in North Africa, and the Germans suffered a disastrous defeat at Stalingrad (above). For the first time since the threatened enemy invasion in 1940, church bells rang out in England – notably from Coventry Cathedral, where the spire was the only part of the building left standing. 'Did you hear them in occupied Europe?' asked a BBC radio announcer. 'Did you hear them in Germany?'

The Royal Family saved petrol as they inspected the August harvest at Sandringham (below). A splendid crop of oats had been grown across the King's private golf course. Other propaganda poses (right) were less convincing. Italy's surrender (left) was one more sign that the tide of war was turning – and life at home took on a more relaxed tempo. Signposts reappeared in rural areas and the first wartime race meeting was held at Ascot. Penicillin was revealed as one of the Allies' secret weapons, saving thousands of soldiers' lives, and doctors debated plans for a national health service. But there were also signs of more radical change. Indian sentiment was increasingly anti-British as the imprisoned Mahatma Gandhi fasted to the brink of death; and in Britain the Church condemned an alarming rise in venereal disease, pointing to a sharp wartime increase in sexual promiscuity.

Monty is Leading the Great Assault on Europe
ALLIES INVADE FRANCE
4,000 Ships and Thousands of Other Craft Take Our Army Across Channel: 11,000 Planes

In a desperate move, Hitler opened the year by ordering the mobilisation of German children over the age of 10. In Britain, April saw the arrival of Pay As You Earn taxation along with the 'Prefab', a mass manufactured home designed for demobilised servicemen and bombed-out families. Rationing eased. The government announced there would be lemons for Shrove Tuesday pancakes, while the end of cloth rationing would mean a return to pleats, turn-ups and double-breasted jackets. In New York, scientists identified DNA (deoxyribo nucleic acid), the basic constituent of the human gene.

When the royal family appeared (right) with Winston Churchill on the balcony of Buckingham Palace to celebrate victory in Europe on May 8, 1945, the cheering crowds called them back no fewer than eight times. There were crimson drapes over the balcony, but the palace windows were still obscured by blackout shutters. Three months later the first atomic bomb obliterated the Japanese city of Hiroshima, ending the war in the Pacific, but also stimulating a nuclear arms race and the Cold War standoff. This new world order took on a sinister dimension when viewed through the perspective of *Animal Farm*, George Orwell's 1945 fable of totalitarianism: 'All animals are equal, but some are more equal than others.' In July a general election landslide brought Labour to power in Britain under the leadership of Clement Attlee.

Queen Elizabeth

1946 ~ 1952

With the coming of peace, Queen Elizabeth finally had the chance to do the job properly. When she travelled with her husband (right) to the first post-war state opening of Parliament, it was like a second coronation. For a lady with an unashamed nostalgia for the grandeur of the past, she had a cunning way of smiling at change and upheaval.

Austerity, the end of the empire, the Cold War – the challenges kept coming, and Queen Elizabeth welcomed them all in her glittering but fundamentally classless style. Labour ministers and Trade Union leaders found themselves dancing the conga with her up and down the staircases of Windsor castle, their anti-monarchist suspicions quite dissipated by the jollity of the Glamis-style house parties that she organised for the new Establishment. When an Afrikaaner told her bluntly in 1947 that he could never quite forgive the English for having conquered his country, she told him she could understand that perfectly: 'We feel very much the same in Scotland.'

She soothed her tired husband's anxieties on that 1947 royal tour of South Africa, and later in the year there was all the excitement of her elder daughter's marriage to Prince Philip of Greece. She found more time for gardening with Bertie, and in April 1948, the couple celebrated their silver wedding, driving in an open State landau through London streets that were thronged with cheering crowds.

But the King's health was frail. Heavy smoking and years of unremitting worry had taken their toll. Cancer was diagnosed, and his Christmas broadcast for 1951 had to be recorded in sections. He was too weak to read it right the way through – and suddenly Elizabeth was a widow. King George VI died in his sleep in Sandringham on February 6, 1952, aged 56, while his elder daughter was representing him on a tour of East Africa.

The courtiers were helpful, but it fell on the widow to hold the fort until her daughter reached home, sort out the funeral arrangements and make sure that the right telegrams were sent. 'Poor lady,' said Kemp, one of her faithful pages. 'She never had time to cry.'

October 26, 1948. Queen Elizabeth and King George VI ride together to the first state opening of Parliament since 1938

Hitler's deputy, Martin
Borman, escaped and was never
found. But Hermann Goering
committed suicide, and
Germany's other Nazi leaders
were executed at Nuremberg
(top). As Russian armies
occupied Eastern Europe,
Winston Churchill warned of
an 'Iron Curtain' descending
over the continent. British
MPs sang the *Red Flag* in the
House of Commons to cheer
the new Labour government's
nationalisation programme.
Health Minister Aneurin Bevan
announced that tuberculosis
and venereal disease would be
prime targets of the country's
new National Health System.
Hungarian journalist Ladislao
Biro invented the ball-point
pen, and Queen Elizabeth
relaxed with her family (right)
at Royal Lodge, Windsor.
Her Majesty could take quiet
pleasure from an innovation
proposed by the Jockey
Club – racecourse cameras
to decide 'photo-finishes'.

The Queen and King celebrated the marriage of their daughter Elizabeth to Prince Philip (left) and enjoyed sun and ceremony on their Royal Tour of South Africa (above and right). It was goodbye to Empire when Pakistan and India won their independence in August, 1947, amid tragic violence (right). In Palestine, Jews took up arms to proclaim the State of Israel on May 14, 1948. A daily shuttle of Allied cargo planes defied the Soviet blockade of Berlin. In the US, 56 per cent of husbands responding to the Kinsey Report said they had been unfaithful to their wives.

1949

Chancellor of the Exchequer Stafford Cripps devalued the pound (left) and imposed still stricter rationing restrictions on Britain. London's Tate Gallery re-opened following the earlier example of the Royal Opera House (above), where the Princesses Elizabeth and Margaret had joined their parents and Queen Mary to watch *The Sleeping Beauty*. In Peking, Mao Tse-tung declared China a Communist republic.

1950

1951

When the combined armies of China and North Korea crossed the 38th Parallel into South Korea on New Year's Day, America and Britain rushed to repel the Communist invasion (opposite). In Washington Senator Joseph McCarthy alleged that 205 'Commies' had infiltrated the State Department, and swore to cleanse America of the Red menace. In Chicago surgeons performed the world's first kidney transplant. In London Frank Sinatra's debut concert was a sell-out and Sainsbury's opened their first self-service store. The government ended soap rationing – but not soon enough to stop Winston Churchill's Tories getting elected next year (left) by a country that was sick of austerity. Britain had its own Red scare when suspected spies Guy Burgess and Donald Maclean went missing. 'Are you sitting comfortably?' enquired the BBC's new programme 'Listen with Mother'. King George VI and Queen Elizabeth opened the Festival of Britain – a celebration of the return of prosperity – on the South Bank of the river Thames, but it was one of the King's last public appearances. In September, 1951, George VI, underwent an operation in Buckingham Palace for the removal of a lung.

A sorrowing family group of three Queens—Elizabeth the Second, Queen Mary and the Queen Mother—stand at the entrance to Westminster Hall as the King's coffin is carried past them for the Lying-in-State. On the right is Princess Margaret.

Five days after the death of King George VI, his widow stood (far right) watching her husband's coffin leave the royal train that had brought him from Sandringham, Norfolk, to London. Later that day she joined her daughter, now Queen Elizabeth II, and her mother-in-law Queen Mary (above), as the King was borne into Westminster Hall for his Lying-in-State. In the next three days more than 300,000 people filed past the coffin. In America, General Dwight D. Eisenhower retired from the army to begin his successful run for the Presidency, seconded by a young California senator, Richard M. Nixon. Trans World Airlines introduced a lower-priced category of service – Tourist Class. In Britain, Brylcreemed cricketer Denis Compton scored his 100th century, and the new 'zebra' crossings for pedestrians were marked by orange beacons that blinked. In Jordan, the crown passed to Prince Hussein, still a Harrow schoolboy. France struggled to hold back nationalist leader Ho Chi Minh in Vietnam, while Luxembourg saw the inauguration of the European Coal and Steel Community – forerunner of Europe's Common Market.

Queen Mother

'It is difficult to grasp the fact that he has left us,' Queen Elizabeth wrote to General Eisenhower shortly after her husband's death. 'One cannot imagine life without him, but one must carry on as he would wish.'

In her extraordinarily long and sunny widowhood – nearly half of her life – Queen Elizabeth would never forget 'the King', as she always referred to her late husband, as if in the present tense. She marked the anniversary of his death every year with a vigil in Royal Lodge, the home in Windsor Great Park where they spent so many carefree weekends. The two desks at which they had worked together were left to stand side-by-side. Shortly after George VI's funeral, a relative complimented the widow on the cheerfulness with which she was bearing her loss.

'Not in private,' Queen Elizabeth replied.

Then Cecil Beaton brought his camera round again and, ever the trouper, she worked out a fresh role for herself in the new Elizabethan age. She became an indefatigable traveller, representing Britain and the crown abroad, and at home she lived with rare style. In 1953 she moved into Clarence House – the cream stucco mansion a few hundred yards down the Mall from Buckingham Palace where Elizabeth and Philip had been living – and she filled it with flowers, liveried retainers and paintings.

In her second half-century, the Queen Mother consolidated her reputation as the royal family's most consistent patron of the arts. She made Clarence House the last grand private household in London, where life could be lived with all the splendour and opulence of her childhood. When reports surfaced of the size of her bank overdraft, many considered it money well spent, for while ordinary life in Britain became ever more egalitarian, the aristocratic flourish of the Queen Mum paradoxically increased in appeal.

The idea was once mooted that she might be sent on assignment to Canada or Australia for a few years, in the way that royals used to serve terms in the Dominions as Governors-General. But Elizabeth II would not hear of it.

'Oh, no,' she said. 'We could not possibly do without Mummy.'

Cecil Beaton's photograph of Queen Elizabeth wearing one of her favourite pieces of jewellery, Queen Victoria's diamond tassle brooch

1953

News that Everest had been conquered (left) arrived in London on June 2, just hours before Elizabeth II's coronation – though the reports failed to note the words of Sherpa Tensing to New Zealander Edmund Hillary as the two men reached the top of the world's highest mountain: 'We done the bugger!' Queen Mary died a few weeks before the coronation, leaving the position of royal matriarch to the new Queen Mother, who took charge of her grandchildren, Anne and Charles (above), when Elizabeth II left on her six-month tour of the Commonwealth. In Kenya, Mau Mau terrorists attacked white farmers. Stalin died in Russia, and in Yugoslavia Josip Broz Tito became President of a new Communist republic. A vaccine to defeat polio was tested, and, in the absence of clean air laws, smog masks were prescribed on the NHS to combat the hazards of 'pea-souper' fogs.

Left: Buckingham Palace,
Coronation Day, June 2, 1953.
From left to right: Princess
Alexandra, Prince Michael of
Kent, Princess Marina Duchess
of Kent, Princess Margaret,
the Duke of Gloucester,
Queen Elizabeth II, the Duke
of Edinburgh, Queen Elizabeth
the Queen Mother, the Duke
of Kent, the Princess Royal
(sister of George VI), the
Duchess of Gloucester,
Prince William and Prince
Richard of Gloucester.

1955

The hydrogen bomb which America tested at Bikini Atoll in the Pacific (top) was 600 times more powerful that the 'A' bomb that destroyed Hiroshima. More constructive was IBM's 1954 transfer of the electronic brain from science laboratory to the workplace as a 'computer' for business use. *Rock Around the Clock* was top of the hit parade in October 1954 when the Queen Mother visited New York's Empire State building (right). When she arrived home, she had to counsel her younger daughter as the Princess ended her romance with divorcee Peter Townsend (above).

In March Soviet Premier Nikita Khrushchev denounced Stalin's repressive ways, but in October his reaction when Hungary bid for freedom (left) was to send in tanks. Western response was muted: Britain and France had just invaded Suez. In September 1957, President Eisenhower stirred anger in America's South when troops escorted black children to school in Little Rock, Arkansas; but next month the US was united, if only in anxiety: Russia's 'Sputnik' (below) gave the Soviets a dramatic lead in the space race.

1957

NOW ON SALE
NEWS CHRONICLE
DAILY DISPATCH
FOOTBALL
ANNUAL

News Chronicle
Daily Dispatch

JAY IS
No. 1
Page Four

HONOLULU TO ICELAND—'97% OF THE TIME BELOW THE SURFACE'

UNDER THE NORTH POLE
Nautilus makes 1,800-mile Arctic dive

My story:
I don't
want
to brag
by
THE CAPTAIN

They watched
Polar ice
by TV

From BRUCE ROTHWELL: New York, Friday

Army can't
manage it
all, says
Templer

2,500
must
stay on
holiday

CUTTING DISTANCES

SCOTTISH
SUNDAY EXPRESS
DUNDEE

FEBRUARY 22 1959

Powered by LORD BEAVERBROOK

PRICE 4d

Hat-waving, banqueting, the red carpet, and then...

SUMMIT IN THE SNOW

Macmillan and
Krushchev
begin talks

From CHRISTOPHER DOBSON: Moscow, Saturday

'Good luck, comrades'

NYASALAND RIOTS: GOVERNOR'S WARNING

Scots minister tries

Mrs. DENE
TO SEE
TERRY IN

Latest News

THE
STAR
NEWS DESK FLE 5000   Small-Ads FLE 1000

LATE FINAL

NOW, HRH
Mrs JONES

FRIDAY, MAY 6, 1960

Tuppence Halfpenny

The smile of a woman on her great day. The story of the Abbey service, Page Three. More
pictures, Pages 11, 15, 16, 17 and 21. Norman Hartnell's own sketches of the bride's and
bridesmaids' dresses, Page 18. Hour-by-hour new editions of The Star will bring you the
whole wonderful pageantry in pictures and special stories.

The daring sub-polar voyage of the US nuclear submarine Nautilus (left) demonstrated America's potential to launch missiles from the Arctic. Next year saw Fidel Castro seize power in Cuba, while Russia's 'Mr K' invited Britain's Prime Minister Harold Macmillan (middle left) for arms control talks in Moscow. 'Affluence' was the buzz word as the 1950s ended, with Britain's first motorway opening in 1959, and parking meters sprouting in London's Mayfair. British inventors unveiled the Hovercraft, the stereo hi-fi, and the Austin/ Morris Mini. The same year also saw the opening of the first airport duty-free shop. 'You've never had it so good,' boasted 'Supermac' as he won re-election that October. Britain's own swinging princess ushered in the swinging sixties when she married photographer Anthony Armstrong-Jones (lower left), and in November, 1960, Lady Chatterley and her lover were accepted into polite society when an Old Bailey jury ruled that D.H. Lawrence's novel, banned for thirty years, was not obscene. In the United States, John Fitzgerald Kennedy, 43, won election as the country's youngest-ever President – and in Rome an 18-year-old light-heavyweight called Cassius Clay danced his first steps to being 'the greatest' when he won an Olympic gold medal. As she enjoyed herself at London's Grosvenor House Hotel (right), Britain's most active grandmother was also staying light on her feet.

While Yuri Gagarin circled the earth (top), the birth control pill went on sale in Britain, Nazi Adolf Eichmann went on trial in Jerusalem, and East Germany built its Wall across Berlin. In 1962, the world came to the brink of war (above), Nelson Mandela was sent to prison in South Africa, Marilyn Monroe was found dead, and JFK sent more military 'advisers' to Vietnam.

1963

ASSASSIN'S GUN BLAZES IN DALLAS
EXTRA **THE DAILY MAIL** EXTRA
KENNEDY IS SLAIN!
TEXAS GOVERNOR GUNNED DOWN
LYNDON JOHNSON BE PRESIDENT

1965

DAILY EXPRESS
THE DEATH OF CHURCHILL

1964

Melody Maker
DIONNE WARWICK · LULU
DUSTY · CLIFF RICHARD
JIMMY SAVILE · MILLIE
POP POLL WINNERS!
WORLD! STONES TOPS IN BRITAIN!
THE FANTABULOUS JAZZ JAMBOREE!

1966

Daily Mirror
'Calculated, cruel murders,' says judge
BRADY AND HINDLEY GO TO JAIL FOR LIFE
IAN BRADY   MYRA HINDLEY
Watery beer upsets an MP

One Sunday morning in the early 1960s the Queen Mother was up with the dawn.
A battalion of the Black Watch had been camping down the glen from Birkhall, her home on the Balmoral estate in Scotland, and she wanted to greet them as they marched on their way. The Black Watch was particularly dear to her heart – three of her brothers had served in the regiment – so she was waiting for the soldiers as they reached the top of nearby Capel Mounth. The mist was starting to clear when she drove down the mountain afterwards, and she stopped to look at the sun sparkling on Loch Muick. 'Now isn't this the most wonderful view in the world?' she said.

104

1967

A kiss from the Queen Mother brought some thaw to ancient frostiness when she greeted the Duke of Windsor and his Duchess (top) at a London ceremony commemorating Queen Mary in June, 1967. That month saw Israel triumph in the Six-Day War (above left), and in October

1968

Britain's 'permissive society' swung ever cooler with the legalising of abortion. *Let's Go To San Francisco* was the year's theme song, and home-grown hippies took their beads and bells to the three-day 'Festival of Flower Children', Woburn's precursor of Woodstock. The Pope's 1968 Encyclical,

1969

Of Human Life, condemned artificial contraception (above centre), but the sexual revolution swept on. In 1969 Neil Armstrong took his 'giant step for mankind' (above), closely monitored in Britain by the Ministry for Silly Walks: Monty Python's Circus started flying on BBC2.

Daily Mirror

Biafra's last stronghold is overrun . . and 5,000,000 refugees are left without food

WHOLE NATION FACES FAMINE

Ojukwu and his advisers fly out

WHAT NOW?

The Beatles split up and the astronauts of Apollo 13 only just survived. In Britain, the voting age was lowered from 21 to 18 years of age, and the June General Election produced a majority for the Conservatives led by Edward Heath. Rock stars Jimi Hendrix and Janis Joplin died within a month of each other from drug overdoses.
The Palestine Liberation Organisation blew up four Western airliners which they had hijacked and flown to the Middle East. As the Vietnam conflict intensified, four anti-war protesters were shot dead at Kent State University in Ohio. Civil war in West Africa (top) between Biafra and Nigeria produced tragedy. In Poland, a dockworker called Lech Walesa started organising protests against the Communist authorities in Gdansk. At Royal Lodge, Windsor (left), the Queen Mother welcomed Cecil Beaton for another royal photo session: they had first met thirty-one years earlier to re-create her triumph in Paris (see page 70) – and the magic was still there.

THE GUARDIAN

London   Friday October 29 1971   5p

Tory Market rebels threaten to go on voting against Government

112 majority for entry into Europe

The Commons last night voted for entry into Europe by 356 to 244, a majority of 112. Thirty nine Conservatives voted against entry and 69 Labour MPs in favour: 20 Labour MPs abstained

By FRANCIS BOYD and IAN AITKEN

The Sun 13 shot dead in Bogside battle

THE BLOODY SUNDAY 'MASSACRE'

'Trigger-happy' paras accused

THE LAST RITES

CLOSING STOCK PRICES

New York Post

WATERGATE

- Guard White House Files
- Senate Asks New Prober
- Ehrlichman Knew About The Ellsberg Burglary

In 1972 (right) the Royal Family gathered to celebrate the Silver Wedding of the Queen and Prince Philip: Lord Lichfield, the Queen's cousin, took the family snap. Britain was already committed to becoming part of Europe (top), but had problems (left) closer to home – in March, 1972, direct rule on Ulster was imposed by Edward Heath. In America (lower left and opposite top) Richard Nixon's landslide election victory was marred by the activities of his wiretappers – and by the humiliation of helicopters evacuating the last Americans from the US embassy in Saigon (opposite, centre). Supersonic Concordes taking off at the same moment from London and Paris (opposite, bottom) were the fruit of Anglo-French collaboration. Also in the news – decimal coinage introduced (1971); Idi Amin 'exports' 50,000 Asians to Britain (1972); Elizabeth Taylor and Richard Burton divorce, Arab oil producers raise prices 70 per cent (1973); Heath out, Wilson in, following the Three Day Week (1974); Elizabeth Taylor and Richard Burton re-marry (1975); Dutch Elm Disease spreads (1976).

Great Grandmother

1977~1999

'Ever since I can remember,' wrote Prince Charles in 1978, 'my grandmother has been the most wonderful example of fun, laughter, warmth, infinite security and, above all else, exquisite taste… For me she has always been one of those extraordinarily rare people whose touch can turn everything to gold.'

For nearly half a century the Queen Mother was to play the role of matriarch to the nation, and matriarch to her family as well. Particularly close to Prince Charles, she was the one member of the family to offer him consolation during his difficult school years at Gordonstoun. She provided fond support to the children of Princess Margaret and Lord Snowdon during the breakup of their parents' marriage, and was to become the archetypal granny to her numerous great grandchildren – eight of them and multiplying.

Her longevity is astonishing. In 1982 she overtook Queen Victoria who, at 81, held the record as Britain's previously longest-lived queen. The Queen Mother attributed her rude health to her reliance on the alternative therapies of homeopathy and to a positive mental attitude: if you refuse to accept an ailment, she believed, it would rapidly go away. A stiff gin and Dubonnet also had beneficial effects.

In the early 1980s it became a new national custom for people to gather outside Clarence House every August 4 to celebrate the Queen Mother's birthday. With each passing year the crowds grew larger, and an increasing number of the well-wishers were children. Interviewed afterwards, many were uncertain about the precise identity of the personage they had just met, but they agreed they felt better for seeing her. It served as a timeless example of the royal mystery – and of the royal mystique which she came to embody in a style that was all her own.

Through a century of charm, hard work, dedication and panache, Elizabeth Bowes Lyon was to earn herself a unique place in the affection of her country and the world. Britain has had many great queens, but there has only been one Queen Mother.

The Queen Mother with her great grandson, Prince Harry, photographed by Snowdon in December 1984

Wednesday June 8 1977
No 60,024
Price fifteen pence

Prince Charles on the Commonwealth's future: Special Report

THE TIMES

One million people greet the Queen on her Silver Jubilee Day

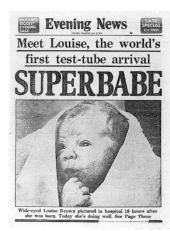

BRITAIN'S BIGGEST EVENING SALE

Evening News

LATE SPECIAL CITY PRICES

Meet Louise, the world's first test-tube arrival

SUPERBABE

Wide-eyed Louise Brown pictured in hospital 18 hours after she was born. Today she's doing well. See Page Three

Daily Mail

MOUNTBATTEN SPECIAL ISSUE

MURDER OF LORD LOUIS

Mountbatten and 17 soldiers killed by IRA

THE NEW STANDARD

CITY PRICES

Incorporating the Evening News

Smiling gunman fires five bullets into ex-Beatle

JOHN LENNON SHOT DEAD

Beacons were lit across the land to celebrate Elizabeth II's twenty-five years on the throne (top). Away from the crowds (left), the monarch, her mother and her sister tried out some alternative royal headgear. Louise Brown (above left) was the world's first test-tube baby, delivered in Oldham, Lancashire, on July 25, 1978. In 1979 (above right) Earl Mountbatten was blown to pieces in County Sligo – and in County Down another IRA bomb brought the total of British soldiers killed in Northern Ireland to 316 since 1969. In New York (left), an alternative voice also fell victim to violence.

In 1981 President Reagan and Pope John Paul II were both shot and wounded in assassination attempts. In Britain there were race and unemployment riots in Brixton, Reading, Hull, Preston, Southall, and Toxteth, Liverpool. But on 29 July, 700 million TV viewers sat down to share the magic of Charles and Di's fairytale (top and right). Next year Argentina's invasion of the Falkland Islands produced an unexpected war – and (left) unbridled delight when the Royal Navy's sinking of the Argentine cruiser, General Belgrano, proved Britannia could still rule the waves.

The Queen Mother, studying Derby form (above) with the Princess of Wales, did not view the mercurial Diana as fondly as outsiders imagined. 'It's not hatred; it's a sort of interest and pity,' the Princess once explained, trying to describe an old-fashioned look that Charles's doting granny had delivered over lunch. When Ronald Reagan (opposite above) invaded the former British island of Grenada in the Caribbean, Mrs Thatcher disapproved, but it won him votes back home. Glasnost (openness) and perestroika (reform) were two Russian words that the West was delighted to adopt with the coming to power of Mikhail Gorbachev (opposite, centre), the new head of the Soviet Communist Party. Soon afterwards, in January 1986, the US space shuttle Challenger exploded (opposite) and an ecological disaster struck the USSR: radiation levels soared all over Europe as the Chernobyl nuclear reactor burned.

DAILY NEWS

GRENADA INVASION

3 Yanks killed, 600 Cubans captured

THE STANDARD

Reagan's stunning victory
as he takes 49 of 50 states

HERE
I GO
AGAIN

★ **Morning Star**

End space
arms race

Politbureau unanimous vote

Gorbachev
elected as
new leader

End party
purge, say
expelled
members

Classical music tribute
as Moscow mourns

Rocky Mountain News

DENVER, COLORADO
Tuesday, January 28, 1986

EXTRA   25¢

SHUTTLE
EXPLODES

All 7 in Challenger crew die after liftoff

The fireball that signaled disaster for shuttle mission 51-L occurred only 1 minute, 15 seconds after liftoff from Kennedy Space Center. NASA officials said there were no apparent problems at the time.

1987

THE LONDON
DAILY NEWS

Maggie makes it a hat-trick
THIRD TIME THATCHER

1988

THE SCOTSMAN

Jumbo in horror crash

When artist Molly Bishop was commissioned to paint a portrait of the Queen Mother in March 1988, she asked her friend Sir Geoffrey Shakerley to take some photographs – she did not want her subject tired by having to pose for too many sittings. Shakerley's most endearing shot is published here (above right) for the first time, by kind permission of Her Majesty. Right, the Queen Mother drives with her great-grandson Prince William and the Princess of Wales to the Trooping the Colour ceremony, June 1987.

1989

At the end of the 1980s, the Queen Mother was still carrying out nearly 130 engagements a year – the most important of them on Armistice Day, at the annual Service of Remembrance (above). In 1987 Margaret Thatcher (opposite top) became the century's only Prime Minister to win three elections in a row. The terrorist bombing of Pan Am Flight 103 over Lockerbie, Scotland (opposite middle) was Britain's worst ever air disaster. In June, 1989, China's leaders displayed the ugly face of Communism in Beijing's Tiananmen Square (left), but momentous changes were afoot in Europe. By the end of the year the Berlin Wall had fallen and the Cold War was over.

The new Conservative face for the 90s, 47-year-old John Major (left) dropped Mrs Thatcher's Poll Tax and tried to make better friends with Europe. The invasion of Kuwait by Iraq's Saddam Hussein (below) provoked a war that made great television and added bite to the RAF flypast on the Queen's birthday (right). But the Gulf War was won by old-fashioned ground forces. On Christmas Day, 1991, Mikhail Gorbachev phoned Washington to say goodbye. The republics of the old Soviet Union were going their separate ways.

U.S.-LED forces in the Gulf attacked targets in Kuwait and Iraq and the "liberation of Kuwait has begun," the White House announced today.

Spokesman Marlin Fitzwater told reporters President George Bush would make a statement to the American people at 9 pm EST (0200 GMT).

"The liberation of Kuwait has begun," Fitzwater said.

"In conjunction with the forces of our coalition partners, the U.S. has moved under the code name 'Operation Desert Storm,' to enforce the mandates of the UN Security Council," he said.

"As of 7 pm Eastern Standard Time (midnight GMT), Operation Desert Storm forces were engaging targets in Kuwait and Iraq," Fitzwater said.

The advent of hostilities began less than a day after a UN deadline passed for Iraq to withdraw from Kuwait or face attack from U.S.-led forces massed in the Gulf.

White House officials said key members of Congress were notified shortly before the at-

tack began.

CBS television reported that a steady cresting near air bases there.

Reporters had been ordered to go inside and advised to put on their gas masks. An ABC correspondent filed from Saudi Arabia said a military spokesman in central Saudi Arabia said the fighting started when the first F-15E fighterbombers took off at 12:50 am local time (2150 GMT).

Colonel Ray Davies, chief maintenance officer of the base, said: "This is history in the making."

"It's absolutely awesome. The ground shook and you felt it," said Davies. "We've been waiting here for five months now. Now we finally got to do what we were sent to do."

CNN reported that Baghdad "has gone black."

ABC reported from Saudi Arabia that air raid sirens had been

turned 'on' and 'were screaming near air bases there.

Earlier anti-aircraft guns opened fire over Baghdad early today, the American Cable News Network reported. "White flashes are everywhere, bullets are being fired up into the air," CNN correspondent John Holliman said in a satellite blacked out.

"Now hear loud retorts, this hotel is shaking. Baghdad is still blacked out." Holliman said, looking out

over the Iraqi capital.

"We are not sure if bombs now. They just got the main telecommunications centre...the planes are circling... apparently coming back for more targets," Holliman said.

"There is a lot of fire going up — there is no sign that any of the aircraft have suffered any damage...we've seen no sign that have been hit," Holliman said.

"They are bombing from quite a height...no swooping, dive-bomb attacks," correspondent Peter Arnett, reported from the Iraqi capital.

"Thick polls of black smoke are rising from the city...the skies is illuminated now by large flashes...the entire city is blacked out," said Holliman.

"A bomb came down near the hotel...you can feel it shaking the building (the Rashid hotel)."

"There's a very bright flash at a refinery building," Holliman said.

"There's something on fire...an explosion is another refinery under attack."

Earlier five American Awacs surveillance

aircraft took off from Riyadh's military air base. The Airborne Warning and Control System planes were accompanied by three large transport aircraft, all taking off within a 20-minute period.

On Wednesday morning, a total of 14 Awacs planes were

manifest of the Saudi Arabia as quoting a media pool report as saying:

"The (attacking) pilots took off at...12.50 am (2150 GMT) Saudi Arabian time."

In London, the British Defence Ministry said British forces had also been in action.

Dollar soars

TOKYO (Reuter) — The U.S. dollar soared sharply and share prices fell at the open in Tokyo today after television reports that an air raid was taking place on the Iraqi capital of Baghdad.

The key Nikkei stock average fell 154.51 points, or 0.69 per cent, to 22,288.19 in the first five minutes of trade, and continued to fall.

trade on the reports, although some dealers were not sure if the antiaircraft fire was the beginning of an all-out war in the region. But one dealer said: "I believe a war broke out. At the moment, I can't tell how far the dollar will go."

The U.S. currency opened at 137.95 yen and 1.5525 German marks after closing at 136.50 yen and 1.5480 marks in New York yesterday.

Fergie and Andrew separated, Anne and Mark divorced, fire gutted Windsor Castle – no wonder Queen Elizabeth II called 1992 her 'annus horribilis'. She was speaking in London's Guildhall that November, and there was worse to come: Her Majesty would start paying tax, announced Buckingham Palace – and Charles and Diana would also go their separate ways. At least there were handshakes (above) in the Middle East.

At the age of 94, the Queen Mother was still fulfilling her annual St Patrick's Day commitment (left), presenting the shamrock to the Irish Guards. 1994 was the year when the term 'ethnic cleansing' entered the language, with gruesome application to civil wars in both Yugoslavia and central Africa; in America television became a prying participant in the Los Angeles police investigation of football hero O.J. Simpson, following the grisly murder of his wife. But it was also the year when some long-desired dreams actually came true. On May 6, Queen Elizabeth II and France's President François Mitterand took an inaugural train together through the Channel Tunnel, and four days later (top) Nelson Mandela was sworn in as the first black President of South Africa. There was also a smiling new face in British politics. Following the unexpected death of Labour leader John Smith, the party turned to 41-year-old Tony Blair to point them towards victory in the next election.

One hip went, and then the other – so the Queen-Mum-Mobile came in useful for birthday celebrations (above). In 1995 the Middle Eastern peace process received a setback (far left) with the murder of Israeli Prime Minister Yitzhak Rabin, and in 1996 the world bid a puzzled welcome (left) to Dolly the sheep. September 1997 (right) saw a tragic end to a tumultuous royal chapter. Opposite, in Clarence House, a 1997 birthday pose.

The personal misadventures of the world's most powerful man (top) were a universe away from the interests, beliefs and style of Queen Elizabeth the Queen Mother. Her way of dealing with life's distasteful aspects was simply to ignore them – for ninety-eight years had taught her that, in the larger scheme of things, they would eventually fade away. On her birthday that year she was surrounded by her family outside the gates of Clarence House. From left to right: Princess Beatrice, Prince Andrew, Prince Harry, Prince Charles, Her Majesty the Queen, Prince William, the Queen Mother with Princess Eugenie, Prince Edward, Zara Phillips standing behind Princess Margaret, Daniel Chatto and Lady Sarah Chatto (nee Armstrong-Jones).

1999

An old headline (left) from the century's newest newspaper, the commuter daily *Metro*, 'freebie' sister to the *Daily Mail*; trouble in the Balkans, bombing raids, refugees, ethnic tensions – as the decade ended messily, it was difficult to see what mankind had learned in the course of a hundred years. But when the Queen Mother went to St Paul's Cathedral in May, 1999 (right and above), to unveil a memorial to the civilian heroes of the London 'Blitz', the wheel came full circle in a more positive sense, for the ceremony –

and her enduring presence – reaffirmed the values for which she had always stood: stability, humanity, duty, and courage worn with an unfailing smile. In St Paul's Churchyard she talked earnestly with Marie Joseph (above), the 80-year-old survivor of a Luftwaffe attack on Shaftsbury Avenue in 1941. 'Where were *you* when you were bombed?' enquired Her Majesty, and Marie launched into her story – while singer Vera Lynn, another heroine of those dangerous years, also listened (to the Queen Mother's left).

A century of history helped shape Queen Elizabeth the Queen Mother into the personification of all that could make a country proud – upright and stoic, but soft and unmistakeably feminine as well, a mixture of all the qualities embodied in her very particular title. Great Britain has been unique in the world in having a prominent public figure dedicated to living and playing the role of mother, and the decades have shown Elizabeth Bowes Lyon a very rare person capable of playing it – and living it – to the full.

The Queen Mother's Century

1900s

1900
Britain's Trade Unions
fund Parliamentary
Labour Party.
Sigmund Freud publishes
The Interpretation of Dreams.

1901
Queen Victoria dies.
Born: George Gallup,
public opinion pollster.

1902
Boer War ends.
Opening of the London
School of Economics.

1903
Orville and Wilbur Wright
fly a heavier-than-air hine.

1904
France and Britain sign
the Entente Cordiale.
Russo-Japanese war begins.

1905
First aspirins sold in
Britain.

1906
Kellogg's Cornflakes go
into mass production.
SOS agreed as the
radio signal of distress.

1907
British government rejects
Channel Tunnel plan.

1908
Ernest Rutherford detects
a single atom of matter.

1909
Louis Bleriot flies the
English Channel.
Suffragette campaigners
force-fed in prisons.

1910s

1910
In Old California by
D.W. Griffith – the first
movie made in Hollywood.

1911
Roald Amundsen beats
Captain Robert Scott to the
South Pole.

1912
'Unsinkable' *Titanic* strikes
iceberg: 1,500 drowned.

1913
Henry Ford inaugurates the
moving assembly line.

1914
World War I begins.
Britain's Song of the Year –
Keep the Home Fires Burning.

1915
Germans use gas at Ypres.
Poet Rupert Brooke dies in
the Dardanelles.
Albert Einstein presents his
General Theory of
Relativity.

1916
David Lloyd George
becomes Britain's Prime
Minister.
Battle of the Somme –
650,000 Allied dead,
500,000 Germans.

1917
US enters the war.
Russian Revolution – the
Bolsheviks seize power.

1918
Russia's Tsar and his family
murdered in Ekaterinburg.
Armistice signed, ending
World War I.

1919
Rutherford splits the atom.

1920s

1920
League of Nations
established.

1921
Insulin discovered.

1922
Ireland partitioned.

1923
Munich: Adolf Hitler
arrested after
beer hall 'putsch'.
T.S. Eliot publishes
The Wasteland.

1924
Russia: Lenin dies.
London: BBC begins schools
broadcasting.

1925
Benito Mussolini assumes
dictatorial powers in Italy.

1926
General Strike paralyses
Britain.

1927
Stalin expels Trotsky
from Russia.

1928
Penicillin discovered by
Alexander Fleming.
Britain: votes for all women.

1929
Chicago: St Valentine's Day
Massacre masterminded
by Al Capone.
New York stock market
crashes.

1930s

1930
Stalin orders collective
farms.

1931
World's tallest building –
the Empire State –
opens in New York.

1932
11.6 million unemployed
in US.
Roosevelt announces his
'New Deal'.

1933
Australia: outrage at
England's 'bodyline'
bowling.
Adolf Hitler becomes
Chancellor of Germany.

1934
Hitler purges his enemies
in the 'Night of the Long
Knives'.

1935
Italy invades Abyssinia.
Birth of Elvis Presley.

1936
Death of King George V.
Edward VIII abdicates.

1937
Nylon invented in
America.
Building-free 'Green Belt'
proposed around London.

1938
Hitler annexes Austria.
Neville Chamberlain
promises 'Peace for
our time'.

1939
Hitler invades Poland –
World War II begins.

1940s

1940
Winston Churchill becomes
Prime Minister.
Dunkirk's 'little boats' save
the British Army.

1941
Japan attacks US Navy in
Pearl Harbor.

1942
Nazis decide on the 'Final
Solution'.

1943
Germans vanquished by
Russians at Stalingrad.

1944
New York: DNA, chemical
secret of genes, discovered.
D Day – the Allies land
in France.

1945
End of World War II: Italian
partisans kill Mussolini;
Hitler commits suicide;
atomic bombs dropped on
Hiroshima and Nagasaki.

1946
United Nations founded.
Birth of the Biro – the first
ball-point pen.

1947
Independence for India
and Pakistan.
Sound barrier broken –
US plane exceeds 600 mph.
Christian Dior creates
lavish 'New Look'.

1948
Israel wins independence.
National Health Service
founded.

1949
China: Mao Tse-tung
proclaims a Communist
republic.
Allied airlift ends Soviet
blockade of Berlin.

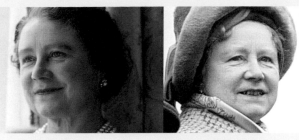

1950s

1950
War breaks out in Korea.
1951
The Festival of Britain.
1952
Death of King George VI.
Last tram in London.
1953
Coronation of Queen
Elizabeth II.
1954
Roger Bannister runs the
mile in four minutes.
Kidbrooke: London's first
comprehensive school.
1955
Disneyland opens outside
Los Angeles.
1956
Nasser seizes Suez –
UK and France invade.
Soviet tanks crush
Hungarian uprising.
Look Back in Anger by
John Osborne, first of the
Angry Young Men.
1957
Treaty of Rome creates
European Common Market.
1958
Manchester United's 'Busby
Babes' die in Munich
aircrash.
Born: singers Madonna and
Michael Jackson.
1959
The Dalai Lama flees Tibet.
Fidel Castro gains power
in Cuba.
Britain's first motorway
opens.

1960s

1960
Sharpeville massacre of
blacks in South Africa.
Soviets shoot down U2 spy
plane.
1961
John Fitzgerald Kennedy
inaugurated.
Rudolf Nurcyev defects.
1962
Andy Warhol paints soup
cans.
1963
JFK assassinated in Dallas.
'I have a dream,' says Martin
Luther King.
The Great Train Robbers
net £2.6 million.
Profumo scandal brings
down Harold Macmillan.
1964
Nelson Mandela sentenced
to life imprisonment.
1965
Death of Winston Churchill.
1966
World Cup Victory:
England 4 Germany 2.
Time magazine hails
'Swinging London'.
Mao Tse-tung proclaims the
Cultural Revolution.
1967
US bombs North Vietnam.
'We're Sergeant Pepper's
Lonely Hearts Club Band.'
1968
Soviet tanks crush Prague
'Spring'.
Jackie K becomes Jackie O.
1969
Man lands on the Moon.

1970s

1970
Death of Charles de Gaulle.
1971
Britain adopts decimal
coinage.
1972
Bangladesh is created from
East Pakistan.
1973
Britain joins the EEC.
VAT comes to the UK.
Arabs attack Israel in Yom
Kippur War.
1974
Major oil discoveries in the
North Sea.
First McDonald's in Britain.
1975
US and Russian astronauts
meet in space.
US quits Vietnam.
Spanish monarchy restored.
Born: Scary Spice –
Melanie Janine Brown.
1976
Wearing seat belts becomes
compulsory in Britain.
Raid on Entebbe: Israeli
commandos free hostages .
1977
Elvis Presley dies.
'Boat people' flee Vietnam.
Egypt's Anwar Sadat flies to
Israel in pursuit of peace.
1978
Polish Cardinal Wojtyla
becomes Pope John Paul II.
1979
Anthony Blunt, Queen's art
advisor – a Russian spy.
Mother Teresa wins Nobel
Peace prize.
Ayatollah Khomeini drives
Shah of Iran into exile.
Margaret Thatcher becomes
Britain's first woman PM.

1980s

1980
Reagan defeats Carter in
US election landslide.
1981
Egyptian extremists
assassinate Anwar Sadat.
1982
Falkland Islands war.
1983
President Reagan proposes
'Star Wars' defence.
First 'Compact Disc' goes
on sale in Britain.
1984
AIDS virus identified.
1985
'Live Aid' raises £40 million
for famine in Africa.
1986
'Baby Doc' flees Haiti.
Ferdinand Marcos flees the
Philippines.
Desmond Tutu becomes
Archbishop of Capetown.
1987
Britain's 'Storm of the
Century' blows down
10,000 trees.
1988
Church of England bishops
call for women priests.
Kosovo is home of Serbian
culture, insists Milosevic.
1989
'Solidarity' rules in Poland.

1990s

1990
Nelson Mandela freed after
27 years in prison.
Poll tax riots in London.
Iraq invades Kuwait.
1991
Kuwait recaptured by
'Desert Storm'.
1992
Serb death camps revealed
in Bosnia.
Fire at Windsor Castle.
Last survivor of *Titanic*
dies, aged 103.
1993
Czechs and Slovaks divide
into separate republics.
President Clinton installed.
1994
£15.8 million shared in new
UK National Lottery.
1995
Oscar Wilde (died 1900)
admitted to 'Poet's Corner'
in Westminster Abbey.
O.J. Simpson 'Not Guilty'.
1996
Charles and Diana divorce.
1997
Tony Blair wins in New
Labour landslide.
Hong Kong goes back to
China after 156 years.
Diana, Princess of Wales
killed in Paris car crash.
1998
Ireland: Good Friday
peace agreement.
1999
New EEC coinage – the
Euro goes into circulation.
Nato bombs Yugoslavia.
Hereditary peers to be
excluded from Lords.
Wales and Scotland elect
regional assemblies.

Acknowledgments

We are grateful to Her Majesty the Queen Mother for permission to reproduce certain of the photographs in this book. A number of people provided help and information off the record. We would also like to thank: Captain Sir Alastair Aird GCVO, Linda Binnington, Emma Bristow, Alison Brown, Scott Duncan Campbell, Lt.Col. P. J. Cardwell-Moore MBE and the staff of Glamis Castle, Alex Coupar, Geoffrey Crawford, Ian Denning, Frances Dimond and the Royal Archives at Windsor, Suzanne Hodgart, the London Library, the late Vincent Page, Jonathan Pegg, Clare Pemberton, Piers Secunda, Sir Geoffrey Shakerley, Michael Shaw, David Sherwood, the Earl of Strathmore and Kinghorne and Edda Tasiemka of the Hans Tasiemka Archive.

We are particularly grateful for the enthusiasm and support of our publisher Philippa Harrison and her colleagues at Little, Brown. Adam Brown was the calm and steady centre of our design and production.

Roger Williams applied his keen eye to the text. Michele Cohen at Graphic Facilities kept the production bright and sharp. Gerald Grant shared his incomparable royal knowledge. Nina Drummond contributed her reliable measure of fun and creativity. Sandi Lacey kept stalwart watch over words, pictures, and the energy of it all. And finally, our thanks to 'Video Vida' for taping the royal programmes that we missed.

Robert Lacey and Michael Rand
May, 1999

We are grateful to the many writers, designers, and photographers who have been producing books about Elizabeth Bowes Lyon since 1928. On the history of the last hundred years, our thanks to Derrik Mercer for his splendid *Chronicle of the 20th Century* (Dorling Kindersley, 1995), and to Hunter Davies for *Born 1900* (Little, Brown, 1998).

Picture credits